Contents

Any words appearing in the text in bold, **like this**, are explained in the Glossary

Sequences

A sequence is a set of things which are in order, and follow a rule.

To predict something is to use what we know and understand to help us guess something unseen. Something which has been predicted is called a prediction.

Much of mathematics is about pattern. A sequence uses a rule to create a pattern. If you can spot the pattern, you can predict more numbers in the sequence.

Here are some number sequences:

Sequences	Starting number	Rule
2, 5, 8, 11, 14, ...	2	add 3
1, 2, 4, 8, 16, ...	1	double
35, 31, 27, 23, 19, ...	35	take away 4
64, 32, 16, 8, 4, ...	64	halve

Use your head

Can you say the next two numbers in each sequence above?

What does it mean?

In the first two sequences, the numbers get larger. They increase.

In the last two sequences, the numbers get smaller. They decrease.

Sometimes the pattern is more difficult to spot.
Spot the pattern in these sequences:

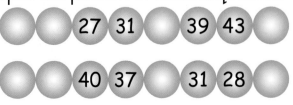

Use your head

Use the pattern to name the missing numbers in the sequences on the left.

Headfirst Into Maths

Patterns

OLDHAM
Education & Culture

LINDHURST		
CHILDRENS		
NORTHMOOR		

book is to be returned on or before the last date stamped.
enew quote ALS number on the title-page and the date due back.

LB.13.12.01

kby

Oldham Libraries

Item Number   A2 868 544 6

Classification JS16

A2 868 544 6

First published in Great Britain by Heinemann Library,
Halley Court, Jordan Hill, Oxford OX2 8EJ,
a division of Reed Educational and Professional Publishing Ltd.
Heinemann is a registered trademark of Reed Educational & Professional Publishing Limited.

OXFORD MELBOURNE AUCKLAND
JOHANNESBURG BLANTYRE GABORONE
IBADAN PORTSMOUTH NH (USA) CHICAGO

© Reed Educational and Professional Publishing Ltd 2000
The moral right of the proprietor has been asserted.

All rights reserved. No part of this publication may be reproduced, stored in a retrieval
system, or transmitted in any form or be any means, electronic, mechanical, photocopying,
recording, or otherwise without either the prior written permission of the Publishers or a
licence permitting restricted copying in the United Kingdom issued by the Copyright
Licensing Agency Ltd, 90 Tottenham Court Road, London W1P 0LP.

Designed by Susan Clarke
Illustrations by Jessica Stockham
Origination by Ambassador Litho Ltd
Printed by Wing King Tong in Hong Kong

04 03 02 01 00
10 9 8 7 6 5 4 3 2 1

ISBN 0 431 08025 9
This title is also available in a hardback library edition (ISBN 0 431 08018 6)

British Library Cataloguing in Publication Data
Kirkby, David
Patterns. – (Head first into maths)
1.Pattern perception – Juvenile literature
2.Geometry – Juvenile literature
I.Title
516.1'5

Acknowledgements
The Publishers would like to thank the following for permission to reproduce photographs:
Trevor Clifford, pp 14, 18, 20; FLPA/Images of Nature (G. E. Hyde), p. 28 (b); Robert Harding
Picture Library (Rob Cousins), p 28 (t).

Our thanks to Hilary Koll and Steve Mills for their comments in the preparation of this book.

Every effort has been made to contact copyright holders of any material reproduced
in this book. Any omissions will be rectified in subsequent printings if notice is given
to the Publisher.

For more information about Heinemann Library books, or to order, please phone 01865 888055,
or send a fax to 01865 314091. You can visit our web site at www.heinemann.co.uk

▲ *Sometimes the numbers around us form a sequence.*

What does it mean?

Sometimes the rule is more complicated.

0 1 1 2 3 5 8 13 21

This is a famous sequence, called the Fibonacci sequence. Its rule is that the next number is the total of the two numbers before it.

Use your head

Can you say the next three numbers in the Fibonacci sequence?

Here are some more sequences.
They do not always need to involve numbers.

1 $\frac{1}{2}$ $\frac{1}{3}$ $\frac{1}{4}$ $\frac{1}{5}$

five ten fifteen twenty

a d g j m

Play the sequence game

You need a partner. Choose a start number and a rule for a sequence. Take turns to write the numbers in the sequence. Keep going until one person cannot continue any further.

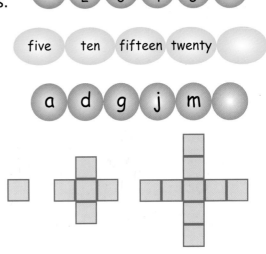

Patterns in multiplication tables

Here is the start of the ×3 and the ×4 multiplication tables:

1 × 3 = 3	1 × 4 = 4
2 × 3 = 6	2 × 4 = 8
3 × 3 = 9	3 × 4 = 12
4 × 3 = 12	4 × 4 = 16
5 × 3 = 15	5 × 4 = 20
6 × 3 = 18	6 × 4 = 24

Use your head

Continue each table up to 10 × 3 and 10 × 4.

What does it mean?

The numbers on the right of the tables are called **multiples**.

The multiples of 3 are: 3, 6, 9, 12, 15, 18, …

The multiples of 4 are: 4, 8, 12, 16, 20, 24, …

The multiples of other numbers are:

×1	1	2	3	4	5	6	7	8	9	10
×2	2	4	6	8	10	12	14	16	18	20
×3	3	6	9	12	15	18	21	24	27	30
×4	4	8	12	16	20	24	28	32	36	40
×5	5	10	15	20	25	30	35	40	45	50
×6	6	12	18	24	30	36	42	48	54	60
×7	7	14	21	28	35	42	49	56	63	70
×8	8	16	24	32	40	48	56	64	72	80
×9	9	18	27	36	45	54	63	72	81	90
×10	10	20	30	40	50	60	70	80	90	100

Use your head

Can you say the next three numbers in each set of multiples?

What does it mean?

By writing all the multiples in a square, we make a **multiplication square** or a tables square.

1	2	3	4	5	6	7	8	9	10
2	4	6	8	10	12	14	16	18	20
3	6	9	12	15	18	21	24	27	30
4	8	12	16	20	24	28	32	36	40
5	10	15	20	25	30	35	40	45	50
6	12	18	24	30	36	42	48	54	60
7	14	21	28	35	42	49	56	63	70
8	16	24	32	40	48	56	64	72	80
9	18	27	36	45	54	63	72	81	90
10	20	30	40	50	60	70	80	90	100

▶ *A multiplication square*

SPOT THESE PATTERNS

- the multiples of 4 are in the 4th row and in the 4th column

- look for patterns in numbers which appear often in the multiplication square. These can be called rainbow patterns.

18-rainbow

12-rainbow

20-rainbow

24-rainbow

Play the multiplication game

Use playing cards with the picture cards removed. Deal out all of the cards in pairs. Try multiplying each pair of numbers together. Check your answers using the multiplication square. How many can you do correctly? Shuffle the cards and try again.

7

Multiples patterns

There are patterns in the position of **multiples** on a 1–100 square.

The multiples are coloured green to show the patterns.

× 2

1	2	3	4	5	6	7	8	9	10
11	12	13	14	15	16	17	18	19	20
21	22	23	24	25	26	27	28	29	30
31	32	33	34	35	36	37	38	39	40
41	42	43	44	45	46	47	48	49	50
51	52	53	54	55	56	57	58	59	60
61	62	63	64	65	66	67	68	69	70
71	72	73	74	75	76	77	78	79	80
81	82	83	84	85	86	87	88	89	90
91	92	93	94	95	96	97	98	99	100

× 4

1	2	3	4	5	6	7	8	9	10
11	12	13	14	15	16	17	18	19	20
21	22	23	24	25	26	27	28	29	30
31	32	33	34	35	36	37	38	39	40
41	42	43	44	45	46	47	48	49	50
51	52	53	54	55	56	57	58	59	60
61	62	63	64	65	66	67	68	69	70
71	72	73	74	75	76	77	78	79	80
81	82	83	84	85	86	87	88	89	90
91	92	93	94	95	96	97	98	99	100

× 5

1	2	3	4	5	6	7	8	9	10
11	12	13	14	15	16	17	18	19	20
21	22	23	24	25	26	27	28	29	30
31	32	33	34	35	36	37	38	39	40
41	42	43	44	45	46	47	48	49	50
51	52	53	54	55	56	57	58	59	60
61	62	63	64	65	66	67	68	69	70
71	72	73	74	75	76	77	78	79	80
81	82	83	84	85	86	87	88	89	90
91	92	93	94	95	96	97	98	99	100

× 6

1	2	3	4	5	6	7	8	9	10
11	12	13	14	15	16	17	18	19	20
21	22	23	24	25	26	27	28	29	30
31	32	33	34	35	36	37	38	39	40
41	42	43	44	45	46	47	48	49	50
51	52	53	54	55	56	57	58	59	60
61	62	63	64	65	66	67	68	69	70
71	72	73	74	75	76	77	78	79	80
81	82	83	84	85	86	87	88	89	90
91	92	93	94	95	96	97	98	99	100

× 8

1	2	3	4	5	6	7	8	9	10
11	12	13	14	15	16	17	18	19	20
21	22	23	24	25	26	27	28	29	30
31	32	33	34	35	36	37	38	39	40
41	42	43	44	45	46	47	48	49	50
51	52	53	54	55	56	57	58	59	60
61	62	63	64	65	66	67	68	69	70
71	72	73	74	75	76	77	78	79	80
81	82	83	84	85	86	87	88	89	90
91	92	93	94	95	96	97	98	99	100

× 9

1	2	3	4	5	6	7	8	9	10
11	12	13	14	15	16	17	18	19	20
21	22	23	24	25	26	27	28	29	30
31	32	33	34	35	36	37	38	39	40
41	42	43	44	45	46	47	48	49	50
51	52	53	54	55	56	57	58	59	60
61	62	63	64	65	66	67	68	69	70
71	72	73	74	75	76	77	78	79	80
81	82	83	84	85	86	87	88	89	90
91	92	93	94	95	96	97	98	99	100

Use your head

Which multiples make
- column patterns?
- sloping or diagonal patterns?

There are many patterns in the multiples of 3.

× 3

1	2	**3**	4	5	**6**	7	8	**9**	10
11	**12**	13	14	**15**	16	17	**18**	19	20
21	22	23	**24**	25	26	**27**	28	29	**30**
31	32	**33**	34	35	**36**	37	38	**39**	40
41	**42**	43	44	**45**	46	47	**48**	49	50
51	52	53	**54**	55	56	**57**	58	59	**60**
61	62	**63**	64	65	**66**	67	68	**69**	70
71	**72**	73	74	**75**	76	77	**78**	79	80
81	82	83	**84**	85	86	**87**	88	89	**90**
91	92	**93**	94	95	**96**	97	98	**99**	100

SPOT THESE PATTERNS

- They lie in sloping lines.
- Look at the numbers in each slope:

  The units **digits** decrease (go down) by 1.

  The tens digits increase (go up) by 1.

- The digit total is the same for each number on a slope.

TIP If you want to know if a number is a multiple of 3, add its digits. If the total is 3, 6, 9, 12, 15, … then the number is a multiple of 3.

Use your head

Which of these numbers are multiples of 3:

24, 37, 54, 17, 255?

Circles show the multiples of 2 and squares show the multiples of 3.

The numbers which are in both shapes are the multiples of 6.

1	②	3	④	5	⑥	7	⑧	9	⑩
11	⑫	13	⑭	15	⑯	17	⑱	19	⑳
21	㉒	23	㉔	25	㉖	27	㉘	29	㉚
31	㉜	33	㉞	35	㊱	37	㊳	39	㊵
41	㊷	43	㊹	45	㊻	47	㊽	49	㊿
51	52	53	54	55	56	57	58	59	60
61	62	63	64	65	66	67	68	69	70
71	72	73	74	75	76	77	78	79	80
81	82	83	84	85	86	87	88	89	90
91	92	93	94	95	96	97	98	99	100

Use your head

Which numbers will be in both shapes if circles are drawn round the multiples of 2, and squares round the multiples of 5?

Number grid patterns

You make a **grid** by joining lines that are **horizontal** (across) and **vertical** (down).

Writing numbers in the spaces creates a number grid.

3	8
4	7
5	2

A **calendar** is an example of a number grid.

June						
M	Tu	W	Th	F	Sa	Su
		1	2	3	4	5
6	7	8	9	10	11	12
13	14	15	16	17	18	19
20	21	22	23	24	25	26
27	28	29	30			

SPOT THESE PATTERNS

- the number sequence along a row increases by 1,
  for example 13, 14, 15, 16, 17, ...
- the number sequence down a column increases by 7,
  for example 2, 9, 16, 23, 30, ...

SPOT THESE PATTERNS

Choose a square grid inside the calendar, for example

3	4
10	11

- the numbers in opposite corners have the same total: 14.

Check for patterns in each of these grids from the calendar.

A
11	12
18	19

B
20	21
27	28

C
1	2	3
8	9	10
15	16	17

Use your head

What is the total of the numbers in each row?

What is the total of the numbers in each column?

8	2	7
1	5	3
6	4	9

SPOT THESE PATTERNS

3	4	8
5	1	9
2	7	6

3	4	8
5	9	1
7	2	6

8	3	4
1	5	9
6	7	2

• The numbers in each row have the same total.

• The numbers in each row and column have the same total.

• The numbers in each row, each column and each diagonal have the same total.

What does it mean?

If all the rows, columns and diagonals have the same total, then it is called a **magic square**. The total is called its **magic number**.

Play the magic square game

You need two players and a large 3 × 3 square. Use cards 1 to 9, one player holds the even numbers and one holds the odd numbers. Take turns to place a card on one of the squares – 'odd' goes first. The winner is the first player to make a line which totals the magic 15.

Use your head

13	8	12	1
2	11	7	14
3	10	6	15
16	5	9	4

Check that this is a magic square.

What is its magic number?

Patterns in nines

The **multiples** of 9 are:

  9 18 27 36 45 54 63 72 81 90

SPOT THESE PATTERNS

• The units **digits** in the sequence decreases by 1.

• The tens digits in the sequence increases by 1.

• The digit total in each number is 9.

TIP If you want to know if a number is a multiple of 9, add its digits. If this total is a multiple of 9, then so is the number.

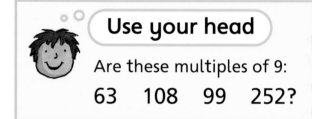

Use your head

Are these multiples of 9:

63   108   99   252?

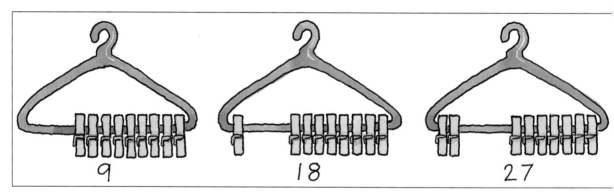

9   18   27

Placing 9 pegs at one end shows 9.

Sliding one peg to the left: 1 and 8, gives 18.

Sliding another peg to the left: 2 and 7, gives 27, and so on …

The pegs will show the multiples of 9.

SPOT THESE PATTERNS

• the multiples lie on a sloping line

1	2	3	4	5	6	7	8	9	10
11	12	13	14	15	16	17	18	19	20
21	22	23	24	25	26	27	28	29	30
31	32	33	34	35	36	37	38	39	40
41	42	43	44	45	46	47	48	49	50
51	52	53	54	55	56	57	58	59	60
61	62	63	64	65	66	67	68	69	70
71	72	73	74	75	76	77	78	79	80
81	82	83	84	85	86	87	88	89	90
91	92	93	94	95	96	97	98	99	100

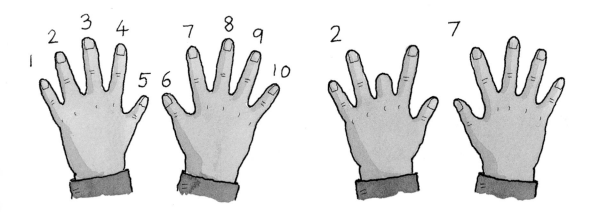

TIP Use your fingers to multiply by 9. Spread out your fingers and thumbs, and number them from 1 to 10. To find 3 × 9, fold down the 3-finger, and count the number of fingers to the left for the tens (2), and the number to the right for the units (7). So the answer is 27.

Try using your fingers to multiply other numbers by 9.

What does it mean?

A pairs pattern is a pattern which links pairs of numbers or objects.

In the multiples of 9, there are several pairs patterns.

| 18 | 81 | | 27 | 72 | | 36 | 63 |

| 9 | 90 | | 45 | 54 |

SPOT THESE PATTERNS

- Each pair is the **reverse** of the other.
- Find the totals of each pair.

Reversing patterns

To **reverse** a number, you swap its **digits** round.

Some numbers look exactly the same when they have been reversed.

44	99	101	353	12321

▲ *These numbers are called **palindromic** numbers. When a palindromic number is reversed, it looks the same.*

mum	dad
radar	noon

▲ *These are some palindromic words.*

◄ *The time on the clock is a palindromic time.*

Use your head

How many other palindromic times are there in a day?

Use your head

Here is a palindromic date. Can you find some more?

29-7-92

Here are some reversing patterns.

For each number, reverse the digits, then add.

| **3** | **2** | | **4** | **2** | | **3** | **5** |

$32 + 23 = 55$ $\qquad$ $42 + 24 = 66$ $\qquad$ $35 + 53 = 88$

(5×11) $\qquad\qquad$ (6×11) $\qquad\qquad$ (8×11)

SPOT THESE PATTERNS

- Can you find a way of saying the total
  without reversing the digits?

TIP To find the total of a 2-digit number and its
reverse number, add the digits, then multiply by 11.

Use your head

Say the total for each of these when
reversed, then added.

43   15   72   41   26

Here are some more reversing number patterns.

| **4** | **1** | | **3** | **4** | | **5** | **3** |

For each number, reverse the digits, then take away
the smaller number from the larger number.

$41 - 14 = 27$

$43 - 34 = 9$

$53 - 35 = 18$

TIP To find the **difference** between a 2-digit
number and its reverse number, take the smaller digit
away from the larger, then multiply by 9.

Odd and even patterns

If you put a number of objects into pairs, then:

- if they pair exactly, with none left over, it is an **even number** of objects.

- if there is one left over, it is an **odd number** of objects.

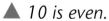 10 is even.   ▲ 7 is odd.

▲ The even numbers are the **multiples** of 2.
Even numbers: 2   4   6   8   10   12   14   ...
Odd numbers: 1   3   5   7   9   11   13   15   ...

 Use your head

Continue saying the even numbers up to 50.

Repeat for the odd numbers.

1	2	3	4	5	6	7	8	9	10
11	12	13	14	15	16	17	18	19	20
21	22	23	24	25	26	27	28	29	30
31	32	33	34	35	36	37	38	39	40
41	42	43	44	45	46	47	48	49	50
51	52	53	54	55	56	57	58	59	60
61	62	63	64	65	66	67	68	69	70
71	72	73	74	75	76	77	78	79	80
81	82	83	84	85	86	87	88	89	90
91	92	93	94	95	96	97	98	99	100

SPOT THESE PATTERNS

- Even numbers have these units digits: 0, 2, 4, 6, 8, ...
- Odd numbers have these units digits: 1, 3, 5, 7, 9, ...

Use your head

Are these odd or even?

546   1327   408

79   3 856 792

There are odd and even patterns in addition. When you add numbers, the answer is odd or even, depending on the numbers you have added.

SPOT THE PATTERN

Use numbers to test these patterns:

odd	+	odd	=	even
even	+	even	=	even
odd	+	even	=	odd
even	+	odd	=	odd

Use your head

Look for odd and even patterns in:

- adding three numbers such as 8 + 2 + 3
- subtracting one number from another such as 10 − 3

Play the odd and even game

You need two players: one chooses to be 'odd', the other chooses 'even'. You both secretly write down any number, odd or even, large or small. If the total of these two numbers is odd, then the 'odd' player scores a point; if it is even then the 'even' player scores a point. Who is the first to 10 points? There is no need to add the numbers; you use the patterns for adding odd and even numbers.

Repeating patterns

A repeating pattern is a pattern which keeps repeating itself, on and on, …

 Use your head

If these patterns were continued, what colour would the next three cubes be in each strip?

What colour would the 20th cube be in each strip?

There are repeating patterns in the units **digits** of **multiples**.

The multiples of 5 are: 5   10   15   20   25   30   …

The multiples of 4 are: 4   8   12   16   20   24   …

If we just look at the units digits, then we have:

The multiples of 5: 5   0   5   0   5   0   5   0   …

The multiples of 4: 4   8   2   6   0   4   8   2   …

SPOT THE PATTERN

- Say the digits above out loud to hear the repeating pattern, and continue saying the digits after those on the page.

You can change the repeating patterns into shape patterns when you spread the units digits 0 to 9 equally around a **circle**.

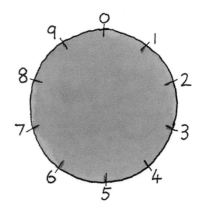

If you draw the ×4 pattern:

4 8 2 6 0 4 8 2 ...

by joining the points at these numbers around the circle,

then the pattern is a 5-pointed star.

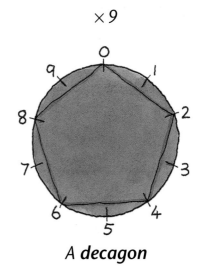

Here are some other patterns created from the units digits of the multiples of:

2: 2, 4, 6, 8, 0, 2, 4, 6, 8, 0, ...

3: 3, 6, 9, 2, 5, 8, 1, 4, 7, 0, ...

9: 9, 8, 7, 6, 5, 4, 3, 2, 1, 0, ...

×2	×3	×9

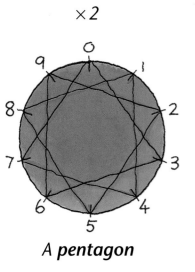
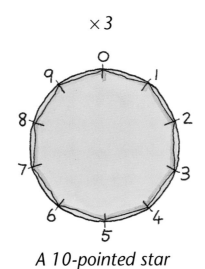
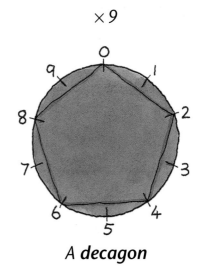

A pentagon	*A 10-pointed star*	*A decagon*

Number shape patterns

You make a number shape pattern by arranging a number of objects to make a given shape.

You make a **rectangular number** by arranging objects in the shape of a rectangle.

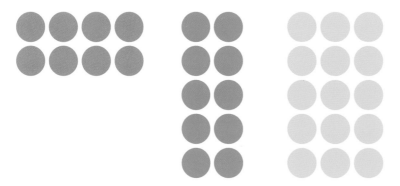

◀ 8 counters, 10 counters and 15 counters have been arranged in the shape of a rectangle.

8, 10 and 15 are rectangular numbers.

Use your head

Which of these numbers are rectangular?

18   23   30   37

◀ The tins are arranged in a triangular shape.

1, 3, 6 and 10 are **triangular numbers**.

Use your head

What are the next two triangular numbers?

What does it mean?

You make a **square number** by arranging that number of objects in the shape of a square.

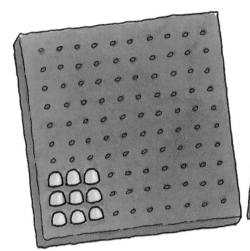 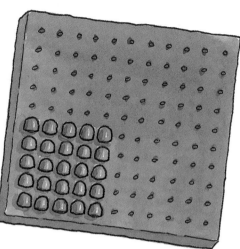

▶ *The pegs are arranged in the shape of a square.*

9 and 25 are square numbers.

▶ *You can clearly see the square numbers in a* **multiplication square**. *They lie on a* **diagonal line**.

The square numbers are:

$$1 \times 1 = 1$$
$$2 \times 2 = 4$$
$$3 \times 3 = 9$$
$$4 \times 4 = 16$$
$$5 \times 5 = 25$$
$$6 \times 6 = 36$$
$$7 \times 7 = 49$$
$$8 \times 8 = 64$$
$$9 \times 9 = 81$$
$$10 \times 10 = 100$$

1	2	3	4	5	6	7	8	9	10
2	4	6	8	10	12	14	16	18	20
3	6	9	12	15	18	21	24	27	30
4	8	12	16	20	24	28	32	36	40
5	10	15	20	25	30	35	40	45	50
6	12	18	24	30	36	42	48	54	60
7	14	21	28	35	42	49	56	63	70
8	16	24	32	40	48	56	64	72	80
9	18	27	36	45	54	63	72	81	90
10	20	30	40	50	60	70	80	90	100

In order, they are:

1	4	9	16	25	36	49	64	81	100

Consecutive number pattern

Consecutive numbers are numbers which follow on after each other. Here are some examples:

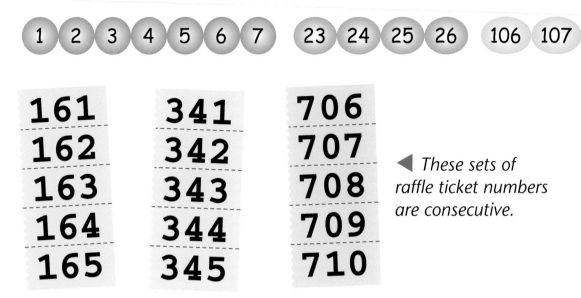

1 2 3 4 5 6 7   23 24 25 26   106 107 108

161	341	706
162	342	707
163	343	708
164	344	709
165	345	710

◀ *These sets of raffle ticket numbers are consecutive.*

Patterns appear when consecutive numbers are added.

14 15   → 29

32 33   → 65

54 55   → 109

▲ *Notice that the totals are all **odd numbers**.*

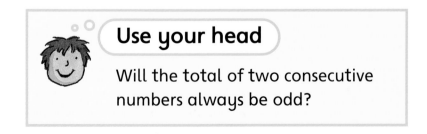

Use your head

Will the total of two consecutive numbers always be odd?

◀ *Notice that the totals are all in the ×3 table, or **multiples** of 3.*

Use your head

Will the total of three consecutive numbers always be a multiple of 3?

◀ *Notice that the totals are all in the ×5 table, or multiples of 5.*

Use your head

Will the total of five consecutive numbers always be a multiple of 5?

These are the odd numbers in order:

1   3   5   7   9   11   ...

They are consecutive odd numbers.

? Question

Do you notice any pattern in these totals?

They are the **square numbers**:
$2 \times 2 = 4$, $3 \times 3 = 9$, $4 \times 4 = 16$, ...

Does the pattern continue?

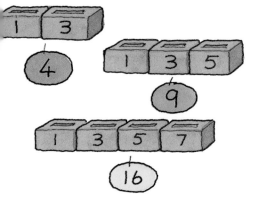

Symmetrical patterns

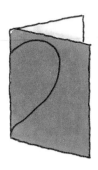

▶ *Fold a sheet of paper in half. Cut out the shape, open the paper out.*

What does it mean?

The shape has **symmetry**. This means that if it is folded along the fold line, one side will fit exactly on top of the other side.

A shape which has symmetry is called a symmetrical shape.

The line is called a **line of symmetry**.

▶ *The patterns on one side will fit exactly on top of the other side.*

Some shapes have only one line of symmetry.

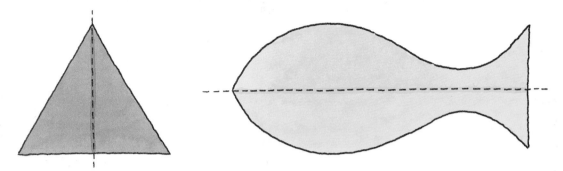

Some shapes have more than one line of symmetry.

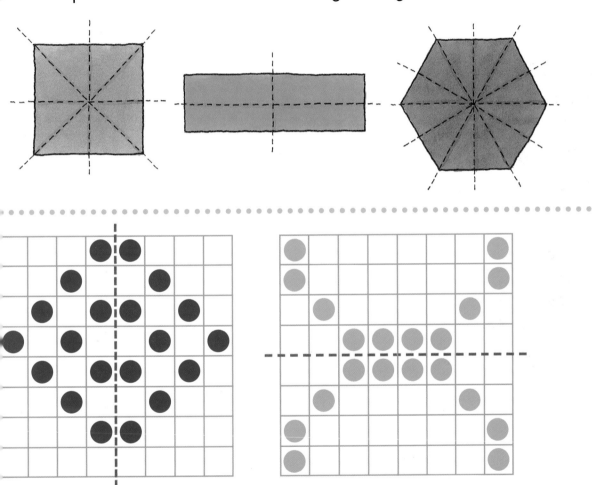

▲ The counters are arranged to make symmetrical patterns.

► The numbers are arranged symmetrically.

4	3	3	4
2	1	1	2
6	7	7	6
8	9	9	8

Rotating patterns

▶ *These are objects which turn round or **rotate**. As they rotate slowly they keep repeating their shape or pattern.*

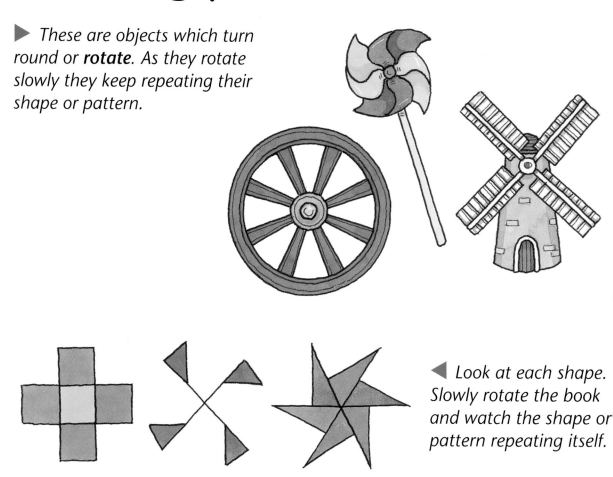

◀ Look at each shape. Slowly rotate the book and watch the shape or pattern repeating itself.

What does it mean?

Shapes which repeat their position during one complete turn or rotation are described as shapes which have **rotational symmetry**.

▶ *Check that these have rotational symmetry by rotating the page.*

What does it mean?

A **diagonal** of a **polygon** is any straight line inside the polygon which joins two corners or **vertices**.

Fun to do

To make shapes which have rotating patterns:

- Start with a **regular polygon**.
- Draw all the diagonals of the polygon.
- Colour repeating regions.

▼ *Focus on each pattern. Rotate the page, and look for the repeating pattern.*

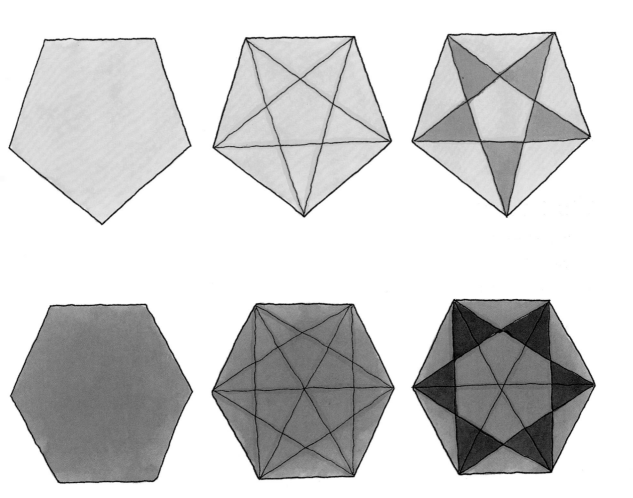

Tessellating patterns

If a set of identical shapes are joined together, without leaving any gaps, then the shapes **tessellate**.

Most bathroom walls are tiled. The tiles must join together exactly, leaving no gaps, in order to keep out the water.

▶ *Squares tessellate. Square shapes fit together without leaving gaps.*

◀ ***Regular hexagons*** *tessellate. They also fit snugly together.*

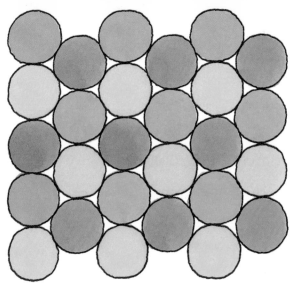

◀ *Circles do not tessellate, because they leave gaps in between them.*

▶ *Cubes do tessellate, there are no gaps between them.*

What does it mean?

A tessellating pattern is created by shapes which tessellate.

Some tessellations use two or more different shapes to create a tessellating pattern.

▶ *A football is made from **pentagons** and **hexagons** fitting, or tessellating together.*

Glossary

calendar	grid containing numbers to show the dates for each day of a month and year
circle	perfectly round two-dimensional (2-D) shape
consecutive numbers	numbers which follow on from each other in order, such as 3, 4, 5
decagon	2-D shape with ten straight sides and ten angles
diagonal line	straight line drawn from one vertex of a two-dimensional shape to another (but not the vertex next to it)
difference	the difference between two numbers is how much larger the bigger one is than the smaller one
digit	symbol 0 to 9, used to write numbers
even number	whole number which can be divided exactly by 2
grid	set of crossing horizontal and vertical straight lines
hexagon	2-D shape with six straight sides and six angles
horizontal line	a straight line from left to right on paper which is held straight; a line parallel to the horizon
line of symmetry	the line which divides the two matching halves of a symmetrical shape so that one half will cover the other half exactly
magic number	the total of each row, column and diagonal in a magic square
magic square	square grid of numbers in which all rows, columns and diagonals have the same total
multiple	number that is in a multiplication table
multiplication square	a 10 by 10 square showing the results of all the multiplication facts up to 10 x 10
odd number	whole number which is not even
palindromic	reads the same forwards as backwards

pentagon	2-D shape with five straight sides and five angles
polygon	2-D shape that has sides made from straight lines
rectangular number	can be drawn as a pattern of dots which can make a rectangle with more than one equal row, for example 12, 14
regular polygon	2-D shape with all its sides and angles equal
reverse	swap round
rotate	to turn about a point
rotational symmetry	a shape has rotational symmetry if it fits into its outline in more than one way as it is turned through a full turn
square number	rectangular number in which the number of rows equals the length of each row, for example, 4, 9, 16
symmetry	a shape has line symmetry if one half can be folded exactly on top of the other; a shape has rotational symmetry if it can fit into its outline in more than one way as it is turned through one complete turn
tessellate	shapes tessellate if they fit snugly together without leaving any space between them
two-dimensional shapes	flat shapes, drawn on paper. They have length and width, but no thickness.
triangle	2-D shape with three straight sides and three angles
triangular number	can be drawn as a pattern of dots which can make a triangle, for example, 3, 6, 10
three-dimensional shapes	solid or hollow shapes. They have length, width and thickness.
vertex	the corner of a shape; the plural is vertices
vertical line	straight line drawn from top to bottom, at right-angles to a horizontal line

Answers

Page 4
<u>Use your head</u>
17, 20; 32, 64; 15, 11; 2, 1
<u>Use your head</u>
19, 23, 27, 31, 35, 39, 43, 47
(increase by 4)
46, 43, 40, 37, 34, 31, 28, 25
(increase by 3)

Page 5
<u>Use your head</u> 34, 55, 89

Page 6
<u>Use your head</u>

$7 \times 3 = 21$	$7 \times 4 = 28$
$8 \times 3 = 24$	$8 \times 4 = 32$
$9 \times 3 = 27$	$9 \times 4 = 36$
$10 \times 3 = 30$	$10 \times 4 = 40$

<u>Use your head</u>
11, 12, 13
22, 24, 26
33, 36, 39
44, 48, 52
55, 60, 65
66, 72, 78
77, 84, 91
88, 96, 104
99, 108, 117
110, 120, 130

Page 8
<u>Use your head</u>
column: 2, 4, 5, 6, 8
sloping: 4, 6, 8, 9

Page 9
<u>Use your head</u> 24, 54, 255
<u>Use your head</u> multiples of 10

Page 10
<u>Spot these patterns</u> A: totals of diagonals are equal (30);
B: totals of diagonals are equal (48); C: totals of diagonals are equal (27); totals of middle row and middle column are equal (27); total of diagonals equals that of middle row and column

Page 11
<u>Use your head</u> 17, 9, 19; 15, 11, 19
<u>Use your head</u> 34

Page 12
<u>Use your head</u> 63, 108, 99, 252

Page 13
<u>What does it mean?</u> each pair totals 99

Page 14
<u>Use your head</u>
00:00, 01:10, 02:20, 03:30, 04:40, 05:50, 10:01, 11:11, 12:21, 13:31, 14:41, 15:51, 20:02, 21:12, 22:22, 23:32
<u>Use your head</u>
For example: 16-5-61

Page 15
<u>Use your head</u> 77, 66, 99, 55, 88

Page 16
<u>Use your head</u>
16, 18, 20, 22, 24, 26, 28, 30, 32, 34, 36, 38, 40, 42, 44, 46, 48, 50; 17, 19, 21, 23, 25, 27, 29, 31, 33, 35, 37, 39, 41, 43, 45, 47, 49

Page 17
<u>Use your head</u>
odd: 1327, 79
even: 546, 408, 3856792

Page 18
<u>Use your head</u>
next three colours: blue, red, blue; orange, yellow, orange; orange, red, blue; 20th cube: blue, orange, red

Page 20
<u>Use your head</u> 18, 30
<u>Use your head</u> 15, 21

Page 22
<u>Use your head</u> yes

Page 23
<u>Use your head</u> yes
<u>Use your head</u> yes

Index